C4648 £4

Crop Circles
Unlocked

by

Jonathan Sherwood

authorHOUSE

1663 Liberty Drive, Suite 200
Bloomington, Indiana 47403
(800) 839-8640
www.AuthorHouse.com

This book is a work of non-fiction. Unless otherwise noted, the author and the publisher make no explicit guarantees as to the accuracy of the information contained in this book and in some cases, names of people and places have been altered to protect their privacy.

© 2005 Jonathan Sherwood. All Rights Reserved.

No part of this book may be reproduced, stored in a retrieval system, or transmitted by any means without the written permission of the author.

First published by AuthorHouse 03/11/05

ISBN: 1-4208-2678-6 (sc)

Printed in the United States of America
Bloomington, Indiana

This book is printed on acid-free paper.

Dedicated to Samuel my son who suffered immensely from meningitis. Better now! His future is brighter.

Many thanks to Busty Taylor for the use of his excellent aerial photographs.

My thanks also to the many people who tolerated my presence and constant pestering.

Table of Contents

Introduction xi
In the Beginning 1
Geo Energy Language 4
Ground Anomalies 18
Pattern Harmonics 23
Design Influences 33
Negative Media 39
Inside Crop Circles The First Step. 42
Hidden Design 46
Pattern connections to Ancient Sites............................... 53
Effects 57
Geometric Architectural energy principles 64
Geometric Makeup 69

x

Introduction

Crop Circles! Are they Myth or mystery, magical or natural?

Patterns appear in the United Kingdom and worldwide every year and have done so for thousands of years and yet, we still doubt their authenticity. Negative media and false claims however, have mainly brought about this doubt, which has over the years totally missed the point!

Crop Circles have a part to play in humanities development and step forward into a higher understanding of many ancient and modern secrets.

From safe and healthy architectural designs to free energy to other remarkable areas of study we find ourselves ever wondering where the secrets of these amazing designs will lead us. Many people have entered and walk out a changed person both mentally and physically in many cases and yet we still have no idea what and how they get there and why they have such profound effects. Why even line drawings of these amazing designs have effects on people who have no idea about what to expect. Then there are the other amazing anomalies that occur from strange events that take place with people who now count in the tens of thousands who state that they experience strange things from absolute quiet inside a design while outside many noises can be heard and yet no noise while inside the design, to other events like energy fields around some designs that can be physically felt as a warm barrier in 3 sometimes 4 layers.

Then there are the effects on the plants and soil inside the designs themselves.

If we are to ever understand what all the designs are about we have to embark on a journey of discovery. There are those who say they create many of the designs. Even if that is the case why do many of the designs have the effects they have which go beyond normal human mental thought and creativity. Some of the strange occurrences that have taken place over the years are many and varied and we hope to cover many of them here in this book.

We can see many examples of ancient geometric influences in both Great Britain and many other places in the world and obviously the ancients held geometric shape in higher regard than we do today! Why?

They obviously knew something that we are not aware of today and here we will search for those answers and reveal them to you.

All of these areas we are about to cover for the first time in one place as we unlock the inner secrets of the Crop Circles Phenomena worldwide.

Crop Circles

In the Beginning

Crop Circles; are they messages from the Gods? Or something else!

In early times, humanity looked at these events as signs from the Gods. Wherever they occurred became sacred ground.

Take places like Avebury or Stonehenge for instance, were they designed after the arrival of a large crop pattern as remembrance of an ancient message. What better way to remember the event than with a sacred monument?
Plate 1

Monuments were built to commemorate the event. The structure would have to take the shape of what appeared so they would attempt in their own way to mimic the shape as best they could.

Back then to build a temple on these sites was the best way to protect it. So the first holy places were created in remembrance of the event and so it began!

Many ancient monuments were commemorated to these types of events and many can be seen in ancient writings in many parts of the world.
Plate 2.

From Egypt, South America, North America. South Pacific, and the Aborigines of Australia. Many of the design shapes are regarded as sacred. In relation to subjects like Maori carvings every curve angle and shape has a purpose. Their entire culture grew without any written language so all their stores and expressions were carved into shapes and flows. The Aborigines of Australia have rock carvings in swirls and circles etc that are thousands of years old.

This gave rise to a symbolic shaping in design with purpose and so intelligent communication with geometric shapes was born. Or was it!

The Maoris have had the ability to create communication using geometric shapes for as long as they can remember and that is a very long time. But not only this, they also can prove that their origins were from Egypt. That being the case it makes sense to recognize that as we have the best geometric dynamic shape of all in the pyramid then the intelligence that understands geometric language must have started there as well.

It is therefore no wonder that each crop pattern that appears makes sense to these ancient tribes of our planet. The Hopi Indians of North America recognize the designs for what they are and we as modern day humans need to embrace these ancient methodologies if we are ever to understand them. But instead we shun and abuse them. Not exactly the way to go! Time out folks! Let's learn to listen for once and contain the arrogance that says we know what we are doing, because we sure don't as we constantly fall over ourselves in trying to understand a very basic principle.

An early scenario with Stonehenge as an example is as follows:

A large crop circle appears in the field and people from far and wide marvel at this amazing event. Identified as a sign from the gods a temple of some kind must be erected to mark the event so a circle of stones was erected.

This over a period of time changes as generation after generation added to the site as a mark of respect and as beliefs developed further. Much like the ancient Mosques and churches were built over earlier sites this event with Stonehenge is no different. Avebury can also be assigned to the same event scenario and one thing is certain and that is that in many cases ancient sites are built over or around some event that occurred in the distant past!

Even ancient tribes such as the Hopi, Aboriginals of Australia, the Maoris of New Zealand as well as the Polynesians as a whole and others understand the crop patterns and their meanings and effects and why they occur. Many though refuse to impart that ancient sacred knowledge to the western cultures, as we are not ready for it, as they understand western thinking processes. And I tend to agree with them as most if not all-ancient knowledge that is more advanced than what we have today either disappears or is turned into a weapon and that is not what this is all about!

Both diagrammatic design images from ancient tribes have a remarkable similarity to crop patterns but we have to remember that the modern day patterns are more elaborate and complex. However the basic principles of the simple side of these patterns is still understood by tribes all around the globe.

Crop circles have appeared all over the world in the past and none more so than in Britain. The reason for the phenomena to occur in Britain more than elsewhere is due to any number of factors but the main one is energy. (Ground energy).

The energy that forms these patterns is complex and yet intelligent and does have an effect on many bio systems including our own internal human systems. In order for it to do this we need to try to understand geo energy language as well as the earth's natural energy system. I am not talking about magnetic energy here rather the energy grid that surrounds the planet.

Geo Energy Language

To begin with we need to look at the Earth as a living cell. With many varied levels of energy, and elements that exist on those levels.

Shape and energy work hand in hand, the ancient people knew this and incorporated that very belief in everything they did. We firstly need to understand how they work and why.

There are many examples of geometric shape playing an important part in ancient knowledge. The best first place to explore would be the Pyramids at Giza in Egypt.

A 4-sided geometric shape made up of 4 triangles joined together in a square!
Diagram 1.

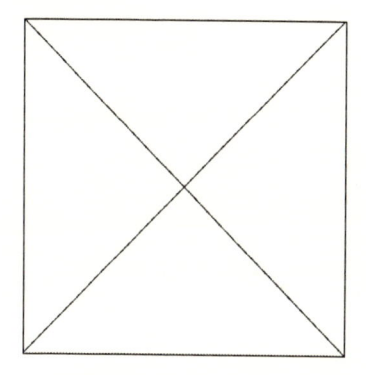

In this next diagram we find the same pyramid design in a crop pattern.

This one even depicts the energy radiating from the apex. You could also say power of the sun, as the source of power is the same universal energy.
Diagram 2.

This however is only the simplest of examples.

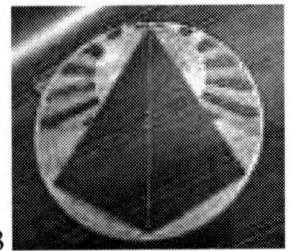

Plate 3

To explain this let's look at a few facts!
1. The sun goes through an 11 year sunspot cycle. This has been known about for many years.
2. The crop circles also go through the same cycle re: their design parameters.
3. The same energy dynamic which can form a geometric shape like the crop circles in the fields also affects the way the sun reacts throughout its 11 year cycle.
4. Interesting though, as evidence has been found in some early mummies that the subcutaneous tissue has deposits of Silica in them. Now if humanity was once a Silica based life form then that would mean that we could not only obtain energy from sunlight but also that extra energy would make it possible for the brain to use a larger capacity thus we would live longer say around 700 – 800 years or more. So the sun being associated with the pyramid shape is not that surprising.

Every pattern that has appeared over the ages for one reason or another has had an effect, both in human psychology as well as emotional and spiritual belief structures..

Both Stonehenge and Avebury in Wiltshire England are examples of early sacred sites to the people of the time otherwise why build them. Their sheer size signifies something large is being represented. Speculation on a variety of reasons as to why they were built abounds, but we all must accept that speculation is all it can be unless we can talk with those who put them there and ask why!

The Great Pyramids for instance have amazing correlations to any number of aspects that point to them being placed there for a reason. And that reason represents a specific level of knowledge or understanding. Also the techniques are beyond where we are today the methods of construction can only be speculation as well, as there are no known writings of the early Egyptians or anyone else building the pyramids. Much like the crop circles claims abound, but no proof is very forthcoming.

As an example the pyramids dynamics point to the fact that the builders knew that the world was round and not flat and yet in the early Egyptian time around 2,700BC or earlier they believed that the world was flat! So how could they calculate the mathematics for the dimensions to portray the world as a sphere?

The pyramids like the crop circles use the same energy both internally as well as externally. So what is this energy?

Crop patterns have been arriving in our time all around Stonehenge and in some cases have had some remarkable affects.

Jonathan Sherwood

Plate 4.

Diagram 3.

Here we see a mathematical design that is created from the chaos theory of professor Mandlebrot's equation. However in this case the image is in reverse.

This design via witnesses we talked to arrived within a 15-minute window by a busy A303 highway in Wiltshire on a Sunday afternoon in 1996.

The pattern is a reflective Julia Set!

But! Why reflective? The reason is simple. If we continue on the path we are on regarding the environment and climate change, then we go backwards and not forwards so deterioration is the direction.

Now the pattern turned up in 1996 and was more or less ignored. Now in 2004 we find the ozone hole increasing faster than was initially thought, the Greenland ice sheet is melting faster than ever thought. (Scientists, back around 1996, thought 1 metre per year. But it is 10 metres per year!)

Ancient sites like Stonehenge and Avebury have always attracted thousands of pilgrims each and every year and one fascinating similarity is that the crop circles attract people in the same fashion. (This is one of the main reasons why patterns like the Julia set appear near major sites like Stonehenge so that hopefully the message will get through.)

This almost magnetic draw to these designs has a fascination to all ranges of people from many walks of life. Many are drawn to them and do not know why!

One reason could be the energy that seems to emanate from each design, and in many cases some more dramatic than others, the geometric shape of the object or structure in question causes this and each one is unique and has its own individual frequency or harmonic signature. Thus some draw people better than others. This comes down to individual frequency types, as we understand the term frequencies.

If we could imagine for one moment everyone on the planet having a specific geometric pattern that, their bodies had imprinted on them, and that each one was different so no two were the same. Then as an individual walks into a pattern depending on the type of geometric design and frequency it was, would depend on how each individual reacts to it.

For example let's use a mathematical identity to explain this, if the range energy types were 23.6666 for the pattern and a person that entered was 16.6666 or 16.16666 then the pattern would have an effect because its range is greater than the individual that has entered it. Whereas if we had an individual that was 28.6666 or 28.16666 then it would have no effect as that individual's range is greater than the geometric crop patterns range.

Either way we are affected by what we see and this makes us focus on ourselves like never before. Every time a person walks into a pattern the design shape and look make us aware of how we feel and that is of primary importance because we are losing touch with ourselves and the way we interact with our planet.

Plate 5.

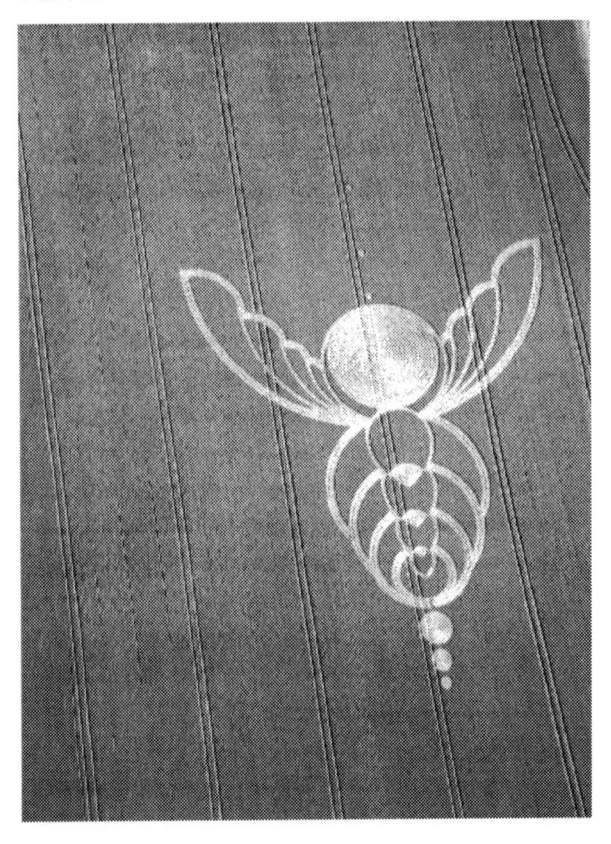

No matter what type of media hype is generated from a variety of sources the people still keep coming, some out of pure fascination and curiosity while others come to investigate and others just to see for themselves what all the hype is about.

We call the energy that is in a crop pattern Geo Energy! This is because the geometric shape within any design affects the energy flow that enters it from the energy field that flows around the planet. Like a lens the pattern then magnifies the energy within through deflection as it is redirected about the internal dynamics, as this occurs, the energy increases in its dynamics. Much like light is refracted through a crystal and the light bands are altered to the expressed result on the other side. Thus the color bands can be seen. This is called refraction.

However in particular designs other data can be found above and beyond just an energy signature.

Diagram 4.

This line drawing of a pattern at Barbury castle in 1991 has hidden information in its design. Geometric energy can take many forms and in this particular design we find 3 elements that represent Air, Earth & Water.

In the next diagram we see the information and explain how it was identified. The resulting variation in octave value represented the frequency necessary to use to separate Hydrogen from water. Plus the variation in alignment of the bottom right element water gave us information relative to degrees as follows:

Jonathan Sherwood

360 degrees equals 24 hours. So 360 divided by 24 equals 15 degrees. 1 hour therefore equals 15 degrees. 60 minutes equals 15 degrees. So 60 divided by 15 equals 4 minutes. So 1 degree equals 4 minutes. So therefore 4 degrees equals 16 minutes.

The variation has an additional value in that:

The water factor is the issue emphasized in this glyph. My analysis of it indicates the atoms used in photosynthesis; carbon, oxygen, hydrogen. The anomaly manifest by the $H2O$ molecule is the four degrees you outline. Light and time must be in sync, so the meaning here is light is unable to reflect through the $H2O$ molecule, disabling the incidence angle of light to equal its reflection. $EM=L2$ if $CV\ [(hv)\ (1/2mv2)] = L2$ Light is the key to the time factor, pi=space/time continuum. What I found in other circles is an $H4O2$ molecule. This molecule will correct the light and time factors and bring harmony to the spheres. Heavy water is source for perpetual energy. The Barbury Castle glyph in 91 indicates the use of the $H4O2$ molecule as an energy source. A synthesis of the crop circle message indicates a new elucidation of the atom. Unless we begin with that proposition, the ultimate message conveyed will be misinterpreted. The circles have given me the structural determination for the atoms. Hydrogen is the only true bipolar sphere. The others are monopolar. It is this mono polarity that will allow the magnetic component of the parallel duality of electromagnetism to harness the atom. Mono polar Technology is the way into the future. They've even shown us the quark and anti-quark of the psi-meson, the neutron. It functions as a reverse bias and is controlled with frequency. It appears you have isolated not only the frequency, but the wavelength necessary to tap into the nucleus. The intent of the Circle Maker is for man to correct the illusion of time, so he may live in an evolution without time.

So in the next diagram we see the way the calculation is done.

Each line joining the circle style is measured and analyzed and the harmonic equation is applied. This approach is done because the overall design is formed on the alignment of the geometry of these lines.

In the wind air spiral at the top shows a vortex rotation of N-. This defines a negative ion rotation of the earths atmosphere at that area is most affected by the water imbalance.

In the lower earth circle we see a negative or N- rotation, which is the earth's rotation around its axis. This appears balanced at the moment so this has not been affected at the moment.

Diagram 5.

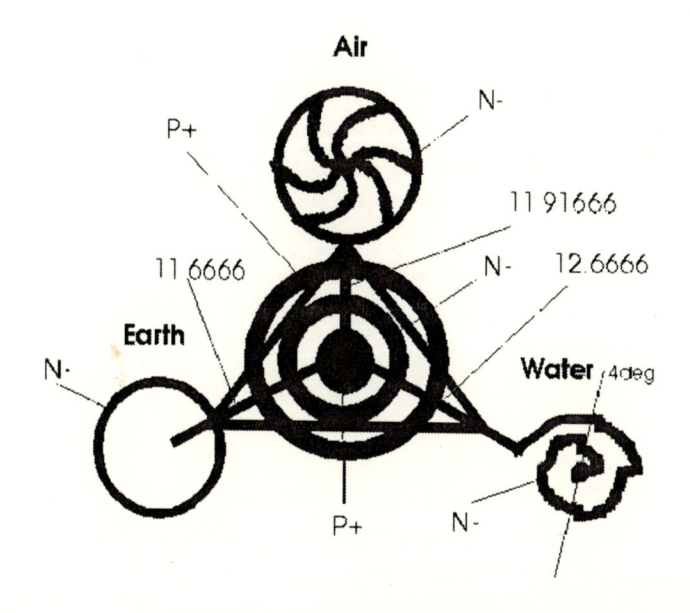

Like the people of old we today are still held in awe at these fascinating designs. The only difference is we do not build ancient monuments to them as we are supposed to be more intelligent and yet we still do not know the mysteries that are crop circles.

How can they have this magnetic quality just from a geometric design?

Why even a simple line drawing on a piece of paper has a dramatic effect especially when they are grouped in sets of 8 or 16.

What holds us in fascination of the complexity of the geometry of the designs and how can they have such remarkable effects on a variety of areas from whole villages being left without power when a pattern appears to aircraft equipment being affected by a pattern as it flies overhead.

Energy? Yes! But how did it get there?

Again we must look at ancient times to help us better understand what is involved and the scientific knowledge necessary to grasp this energy concept.

We know from archeological information that Silbury Hill's internal dynamics are the same as the Step Pyramid of Sakkara in Egypt. So this means that Silbury Hill has the potential to tap into the same energy system as the larger cousin in Egypt.

We also know that there have been many sightings of both UFO objects as well as glowing orbs of light above or around Silbury Hill.

Many Crop circles appear near and around Silbury Hill and there are still many mysteries surrounding this man made mound! We know from research that we had an energy type grid like a fishnet around the whole planet. Bruce Cathie first discussed this in his book Harmonic 33 and depicted the first grid network. Then came Harmonic

Crop Circles

695 which brought both governments as well as military types to become aware of the advantages of being located on energy cross-points on the grid.
Diagram 6.

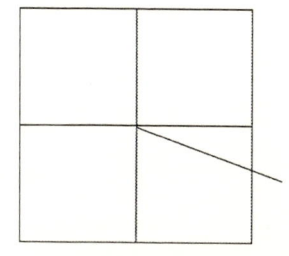

Cross point.

We also know that architectural shapes have their own dynamic energy relative to their height, width, and depth. This dictates how the energy within the shape reacts. A simple square or circle is easy, as there is nothing to act like a lens and magnify the effect via geometric inclusion within the square or circle.

So in a simple circle..
Diagram 7.

We find empty space so nothing to bounce the energy about or magnify it. Whereas if we add a few geometric shapes..

Diagram 8.

We end up with a different effect such as this one that appeared at Overton hill near West Kennett in 2004.

Now we see three swirls or vortex spins that are revolving around a central axis. The axis is formed by both the swirls and the circles own focus point, which is in the middle.

The effect is for the energy to rotate and the rotation is dictated by the geometric shapes direction within. Much like we redirect water around an object.

This process gives us information that depicts a formula that allows access to the dynamic force at work. Housed inside say a circular tube the central vortex is affected by the other three spinning around it thus a dynamic force in between the three is formed as the three curved arms depict in the center point. Tap into that force and you would have access to a perpetual power source of a universal kind. However the shape of the circular cylinder could also affect what happens to that dynamic energy inside if it were changed to something else rather than a round cylinder.

There are various companies around the globe especially in Russia that are now developing vortex energy systems for use as a power source for the future and they do get out more than they put in. Lots more!

Imagine for instance having a power source in a cube shape that seemed to just keep running. This would be using the inner geometric shape within to create that power but you could not see it because of the glow within. It would react to external energy no matter how small as after all we are all energy and it would sense that!

Diagram 9.

Planet energy flow North to Equator

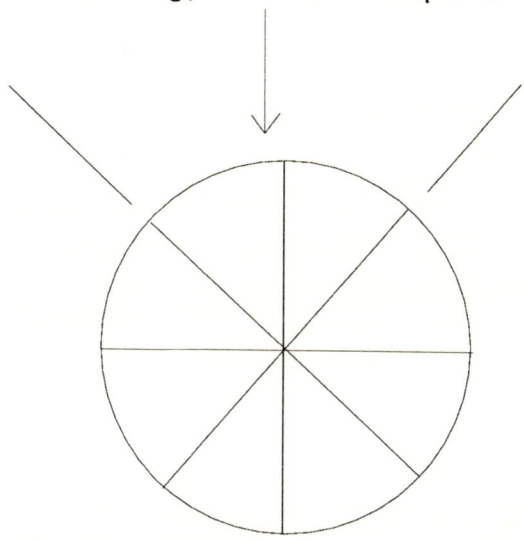

This diagram shows us the way the energy is redirected (Deflection) by the curvature to the center point. This then expands outwards radiating to the equatorial disc. The Southern energy flowing from South to Equator also completes the effect. Two forces at work both dynamic and both controlled by geometric shape. This same result takes place in just a simple circle and yet can change the crystalline structure of a Quartz crystal just by sitting the crystal on top of a line drawing of the shape. Remember we are talking about the same energy that rotates through an 11-year cycle and affects the sunspot activity on the sun. This universal energy is all around us and out in space. Geometric shape is

Jonathan Sherwood

the way forward to discovering the processes to access this energy source.

So let's step further into the patterning process and try to explain why geometric shape is so important.

Ground Anomalies

There have been many reports of Balls of light having been sighted over Silbury Hill and the following day a crop pattern has been found in fields nearby. In some cases reports of these balls of white light floating from Silbury Hill to the fields in question and then behaving erratically in the air for a short time then vanishing as quickly as they appeared. In the morning a pattern is found where the balls of light were just before they vanished.

Connection? Maybe! One report could be classified, as coincidence but over 20 reports seems more than that!

These same balls of light have also been seen around the Great Pyramids at Giza!

The following two designs appeared in the same field. Diagram10.

This one appeared opposite Silbury hill in just the situation we just discussed.

Ground research with radio wave sniffers or RF meters showed a marked increase in the design compared to outside.

Crop Circles

Diagram 11.

This one also raised a few eyebrows when it arrived and again, under the same circumstances at Silbury hill in 2000.

Now let's explore this one for a moment!

We find first the circle and then various geometric shapes within it and one is fragmented! Obviously, if it had not been fragmented, then it would all have been balanced. But what if it was that way for a reason!

Let's run a situation past you for a second! If we had an element that was unbalanced and we knew its geo signature shape then we could mend it by correcting a section of the geo shape itself. But if we wanted to disconnect it then we create a variance of the shape with one part out of shape. We have to remember that geo energy is the result of the geometric shape of an object whether it is a room in a house to a complete building. Geo energy is not the cause it is the result. In order for us to understand the cause we need to go further on this journey into the inner secrets of crop circle geometry.

Early designs were just simple circles to begin with like this one.

Diagram 12.

In early times due to the remains of what we see today we may have seen something like this for Avebury. Diagram 13.

One can only imagine what the ancient people thought when they saw it. It must have been miraculous, magical almost, a sign from the gods. The ancient pathway that connects Avebury to the Sanctuary could have been created due to 2 patterns appearing in the same season. It would make sense to connect them. We have to also remember that their intelligence level then is different from ours today so they would have interpreted the event a lot different.

A similar event may have occurred in the early days of Stonehenge, but with added dynamics included over time due to added stimuli from other events occurring through time.

There are other mysteries associated with both Avebury and Stonehenge. Many crop patterns have appeared near them. Why? There has to be a reason!

Many ancient sites have sacred geometric shapes relative to this geo energy and once we understand it then we can begin to discover how to use it.

One example in understanding geo energy and its dynamic structure is to do an experiment using sound. This is done using what we know of as compatible pairs. That is, two sounds specifically which are compatible in a matrix formula. This formula we discovered in Egypt while on a project there back in 1992.

The experiment would involve a smoke filled chamber with 2 sound resonators on either side of a small platform. When you produce the sounds a helix will develop which rises up from the platform. This will be visible in the smoke in the chamber. At the base of the helix if you place fine sand would be a geometric shape. Within the loop of the helix would be zero gravity. In order to expand this helix you would have to have a sequence of compatible pairs in order to not only make the helix bigger but also to give you control over the zero gravity bubble within the loop of the helix itself. ie: make it expand in any direction to any size.

Crop circles that naturally form are a result of 2 compatible pairs, which merge together to form an energy helix, which has a geometric shape at its base. This science is beyond where we are at present but we are beginning to understand some of it as the experiment above was held in a university in the USA a few years ago.

And the results were just as we stated above. They saw the helix form within the smoke and then with a robotic arm in the chamber they placed a small stone inside the loop of the helix and it just sat there and did not fall to the ground. When the sound was turned of then the stone fell to the ground. Therefore anti gravity was formed within the loop of the helix.

This one factor would give us many answers as to why certain results occur in naturally formed patterns.

But we cannot discount even the man made ones as even they have many strange anomalies occur within them as well as outside of the pattern.

Back in ancient times even ancient tribes would have felt these strange energies and therefore would depict them in any number of ways like certain ochre type drawings by ancient native tribes like the Hopi or Aborigines of Australia, or the swirl type carvings of the Polynesians after all the crop patterns are not solely in England.

If crop patterns are an ancient language then we can only marvel at either its complexity or simplicity for we have as yet to understand one word. We can understand the dynamics and also the power they have. And what about their significance regarding appearance on the ground, from rice paddies in Japan where witnesses have seen 22,000 gallons of water disappear in 30 seconds and be replaced by a crop pattern in the rice field, to tall conifer forests in Canada where the top 30ft are bent to the shape of a crop pattern in the tops of the trees, to the Deserts of Australia and Africa, to ice and snow fields elsewhere in some cases the crop pattern appears as a ring under the surface of the ice itself, these patterns are appearing everywhere!

To say they are all man made is ridiculous, for 22,000 thousand gallons of water to disappear in a rice paddy in Japan and have witnesses as well while the pattern formed is one factor to think about. Then there are tops of full grown tress in Canada that have been affected Top 30 feet bent 90 degrees to form a pattern on the tops of the trees. Then there are the ice rings that appear under the ice surface, all not done by hand.

Even the man made artists have had their share of strange occurrences like time stopping for 2 hours while they create a pattern to making a large mistake and leaving the design for early breakfast to only go back and find the error repaired with no sign of the mistake or damaged stalks where the mistake was made!!

No matter how you look at the crop patterns there is a message there to be learned and we are only now beginning to look more closely at what is going on, on the ground.

Crop patterns have also appeared in undulating fields and yet are perfect geometrically from the air when viewed. This would mean a geometric compensation for the changes in level regarding the undulations would have to be taken into consideration if it was to appear perfect from the air!

Many ground anomalies occur like floating white orbs, small discs with the pattern on then buried in the centre, bent stalks in some cases over 3inches from the ground, blown nodes on stalks, burning on seed head of plant but only on one side, moisture disappears from soil, rains outside a pattern but not in it, all sound disappears inside a pattern but not outside of it. These are just a few anomalies that occur.

Pattern Harmonics

There are similarities with UFO sightings like the Rendlesham forest incident in 1980 when markings like these were seen on the side of a craft reported by qualified USAF personnel.

With any geometric language the inner meaning is hidden unless you know how to expose it!

Diagram 14.

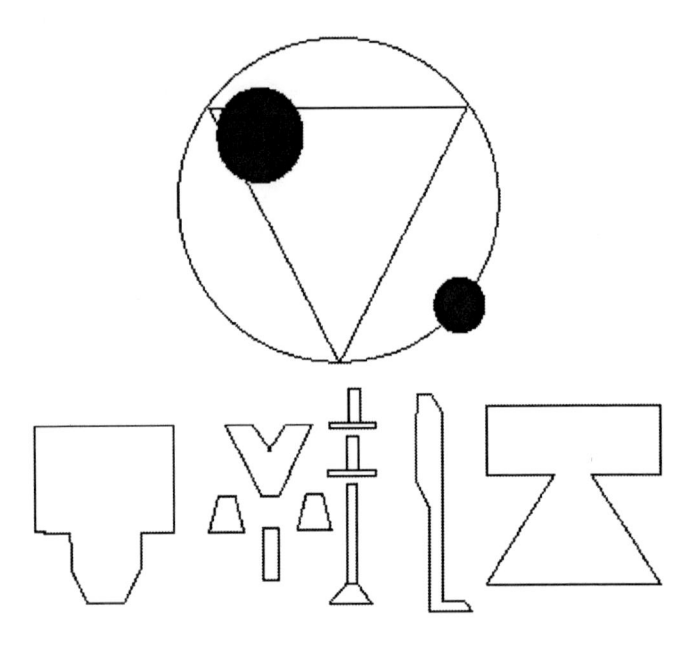

Here for instance we see geometric design that was witnessed on the side of a craft by a reliable witness.

Geometric shape in ancient language can be either cuneiform or diagrammatic. The hieroglyphic language is a good start for a diagrammatic language form.

The sacred art of writing in ancient Egypt meant that the Egyptians believed that the art of writing and reading hieroglyphs, had been revealed by Thoth, god of knowledge and patron deity of scribes. The sacred signs he taught had the power to bring to life the objects they depicted. By painting a word or sentence on a wall, the Egyptians understood that they were creating an animating force that could be harnessed with profitable or disastrous consequences.

Thoth also had the ability to compel matter into form using words of power. This meant that the spoken word also had meaning in sacred shapes in a collective group as well as individual entities. Thus the spoken word in letterform produced a frequency that had power by creating an energy influence over an item or person. Each letter spoken or written has a geometric shape thus the individual letter geo shape had power. When clustered together to form a word the power magnified through a grouping collective process of all the letters combined. Each resonating with the other thus producing a unique energy signature for each word spoken and so thus the sacred chant was born.

Thoth also had many uses for this sacred geometric system both in pattern form as well as spoken form but no matter which one was used they both had significant results.

Combinations of shapes therefore depicted advancement in expression such as the groupings of hieroglyphs to depict a name of a god or other person. This advancement has also been seen in the crop circle arena like in the following drawing of a pattern, which appeared early 1989.
Diagram 15.

As you can see things had evolved from a single circle to a more complex form.

In 1991 a crop pattern appeared that was the first one that made sense to me from the work I had done earlier.

Jonathan Sherwood

Diagram 16.

This amazing design created a flurry of activity with us as the air, earth & water combination was unmistakable. But, it also led us in a direction that we did not expect!

As in this next drawing
Diagram 17.

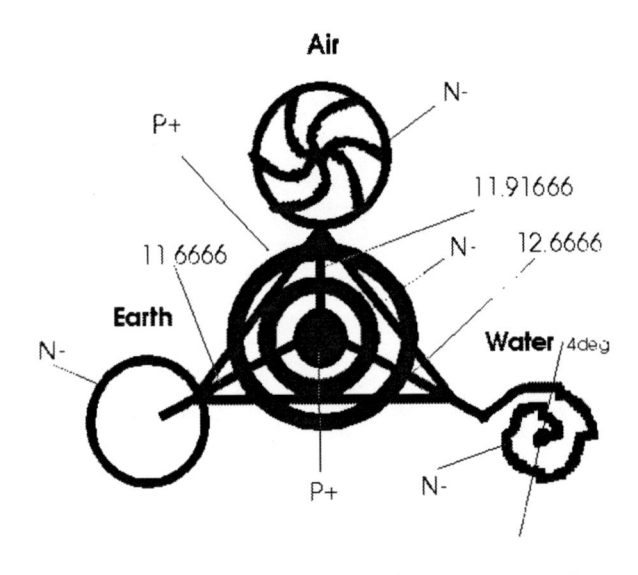

Air
P+
N-
11.91666
11.6666
N- 12.6666
Earth
N-
Water 4deg
P+
N-

we see the design converted using a mathematical equation that is used today that I discovered in 1992 to decipher the energy harmonics of any geometric design.

If we are to understand the technical expertise of the ancients then we must open our eyes to the possibilities that they definitely knew far more than we do today. Many

Crop Circles

examples of our lack of knowledge shows up in numerous ways from trying to duplicate the construction methods of old even using modern day equipment which they did not have, we still fail to match their prowess in construction methods. And yet it is a simple process to produce a frequency harmonic that has the power to levitate any object to any height using the geo harmonic table.

And yet here we sit trying to dispute what actually exists and making statements that it was not done that way and making assumptions that things happen this way according to our so called scientific limited thinking process. And still we cannot do what the ancients did many thousands of years before.

So! Where to from here?

If we are to progress then we all need to open our minds to the endless possibilities that exist in the universe and not go simply by what we think, and use guidelines that are not applicable for the universe in which we live. Time to take a step forward and see what is out there!

Our own solar system has come under the microscope like this next design that appeared in 1995.
Diagram 18.

Grey represents counter-clockwise crop lay rotation!

Jonathan Sherwood

The color-coding shows the different swirl of the laid down crop. This one tied in with ancient knowledge we discovered in 1992. Here is a breakdown of the analysis of this pattern in detail.

The pattern showed a right angle to the earth position relative to the planets of Mercury and Pluto.

THE FACTS

File SEQUENCE NO. C144

DATE APPEARED. 20th June 1995

DAY HARMONIC: 22.16666 (See section on Harmonic calendar for explanation!)

DAY FOUND:26TH JUNE 1995.

DAY HARMONIC. 72.16666

LOCATION. Longwood Estate, Wiltshire.

DISCRIPTION. Planetary orbital rotation map surrounded by 65 satellites, 52 positive, 13 neutral.

SIZE HARMONIC. 265ft diameter from inner point, to outer ring centerline of formation. Harmonic = 22.08333. (Harmonic conversion explained in the harmonic equation section later in this book!)

Total design outer limit measurement 284'. Harmonic = 23.6666. Central circle of inner formation 22ft diameter. Plate 5.

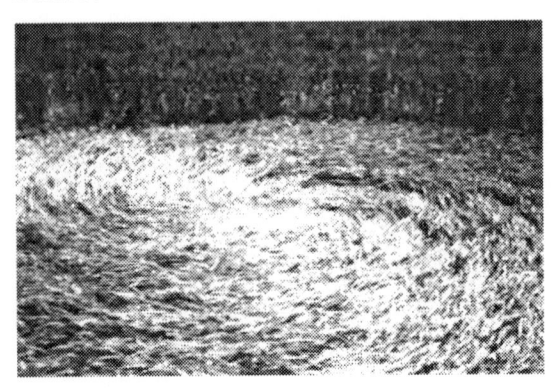

Crop Circles

This shows the flow rotation required for formation to take place. Notice the opposite rotation pattern to the next picture. This means there were two harmonic frequencies being used, as the flows are contrary to each other. Harmonics use reflective forces in reverse so even though the rotation lay of the crop is in a clockwise lay the force to create the vortex was opposite. Thus in relation to the dynamics of the design the obvious rotation of the next line would be contrary to the first. An easy way to understand this is if you take a cloth rag and rotate it with your hand so the rag moves clockwise. But if you look closely the rag is actually trailing anti-clockwise because the force of rotation is making it run opposite the rotation of your arm. So this shows us that two forces are at work in the 144b photograph. Another example is that as the energy strikes the stalk it softens and begins to fold much like felling a tree it falls towards the source of the flow which makes it lay in the opposite direction to the energy flow. In the study of harmonics in our recent research of Egypt we now understand that two harmonic pulses are required in synchronicity with each other to create harmony. Now let's look at the next one!

Plate 7.

In this photograph we see a single rotation in column formation. This means there is a single rotational force, as we do not have a pinwheel effect, simply a single circular ring. Different formation! Which is a simple lateral force of rotation. In this case the rotation is clockwise as the crop is lying. No vortex spin is present as in the previous evidence.

Plate 8.

Here we see the flow around one of the orbital circles within the inner set. Here there are three circles in elliptical orbit around a central mass.

The two outer Satellites show a 90-degree quad to the central one. This is in association to the Mercury - Pluto positions required for the 52 base sequences to occur. Naturally formed energy has to be balanced in order for it to interact and form a matrix which in turn forms a helix with a geometric pattern at its base.

Plate 9.

Here we can see the fine detail in the standing crop. The precision is unique to this formation as it has fine standing lines to form the design.

Let's have a look at some of the research, which connects with this crop design.

Reference to the months of November/December 1992 is therefore required and a correlation to the positions of Mercury and Pluto from the 6th November to 6th December 1995.

Also a reference to Nov\Dec 1992 should prove valuable.

This must be a triangulation with the Earth as an axis.

The diameters of the satellites are as follows:
Top left:16'
Middle Right:8'
Bottom:15'
Inner circle: 19'

If you are an astrologer you should quickly find the connection.

Now firstly the number 13 indicates the 13th Initiatic cycle and this is derived from the Egyptian equation as follows:

Year Code - - Matrix Reductions
1968 = 164..................1980 = 165..................1992 = 166
1969 = 164.08333.....1981 = 165.08333....1993 = 166.0833
1970 = 164.16666.....1982 = 165.1666......1994 = 166.166
1971 = 164.25............1983 = 165.25..........1995 = 166.25
1972 = 164.333..........1984 = 165.3333......1996 = 166.333
1973 = 164.41666.....1985 = 165.41666....1997 = 166.4166
1974 = 164.5..............1986 = 165.5............1998 = 166.5
1975 = 164.58333.....1987 = 165.58333....1999 = 166.5833
1976 = 164.6666........1988 = 165.6666......2000 = 166.666
1977 = 164.75............1989 = 165.75..........2001 = 166.75
1978 = 164.83333.....1990 = 165.8333......2002 = 166.8333
1979 = 164.91666.....1991 = 165.9166......2003 = 166.9166

Fully Reduced Cycle: 1872-2015: 143 year (Initiatic Cycle)
1872 - 1883 = 156 sequence...156 / 12 = 13 (enter Photon
                                                        Belt 150 yrs?)
1884 - 1895=157 " " .....157 / 12=13.08333 (RamaKrishna)
1896 - 1907=158 " " .....158 / 12=13.1666 (Blavatsky, 1.
                                                        Donnely etc.)
1908 - 1919=159 " " .....159 / 12=13.25 (ww 1, Aircraft)
1920 - 1931=160 " " .....160 / 12=13.3333 (roaring 20's,
                                                        Black Monday)

Jonathan Sherwood

1932 - 1943=161 " " .....161 / 12=13.41666 (Great depression, ww 2)
1944 - 1955=162 " " .....162 / 12=13.5 (end ww 2, Atomics)
1956 - 1967=163 " " .....163 / 12=13.58333 (Sputnik summer of love)
1968 - 1979=164 " " .....164 / 12=13.6666 (1972 = E change, Nixon)
1980 - 1991=165 " " .....165 / 12=13.75 (Reagan Bush, USSR fall)
1992 - 2003=166 " " .....166 / 12=13.8333 (Zarlen Equation used re activate. Causes negative cycle active first then positive afterwards. Bush era, 9/11,iraq, Afghanistan, world terror activity.)
2004 - 2015=167 " " .....167 / 12=13.91666..(Arguelles cycle end 2012)
2016 - 2027 = 168 " " .....168 / 12 = 14

In the above we see the Initiatic cycle displayed in the yearly cycle. This is from the Egyptian equation and can be cross-referenced to Mayan, Ancient Egyptian, Inca, and many other ancient civilizations and their texts.

As can be seen from the above scale we are in the 2004-2015 cycle and it shows the 13.916666 sequences. This represents the energy of activation and is used in the initiation of Helix energy through the application of tone harmonics in a specific sequence. This gives us access to sacred areas but only to the initiated and also an individuals DNA frequency must be compatible.

Design Influences

This appeared in a crop design a few years ago! Plate 10.

The Julia set in 1996 predicted the fine balance between order and chaos. This is an energy balance in nature that controls whether we can live on this planet or not. But there is more to this. It also represents the fine balance in human immune systems and that if foreign agents are introduced it will cascade and collapse.

There are many aspects of DNA that are still not understood like why so much junk DNA. Well you do not get Junk DNA. It has a purpose, just because you do not know what it does, does not make it junk!

In energy cycles of harmonic energy you have phases from one aspect to another these occur in sequence first one then the other and one mirrors another. In recent times especially the last two cycles we find some interesting facts.

The first phase is from 1992 – 2003 this is called the mirror or false image phase. This happens in any energy cycle as you rotate from neutral to positive sets and allows for activation process to be initiated before the major cycle begins.

It also has the ability to bring out the worst case scenarios and also can be quite violent in some cases depending on how humanity works through it. But it also has the ability to create illusions of reality. As you can see from the events list previously it was not exactly a calm period.

So that means from 2004 onwards we are into the positive phase, which is where humanity has to face reality. This data correlates both with Mayan as well as Egyptian information regarding the 2012 timetable regarding the ancient calendars.

Each crop pattern has an association with both ancient knowledge as well as hidden knowledge yet to be discovered by us. One thing is for sure we do have to start to look at ways of understanding what the inner secrets are with the geometric patterns that appear each and every year worldwide.

Each time the energy cycle changes we see confusion and change as well as challenge. As with the patterns we should see a similar cycle to the patterns of the last positive cycle but with improvement as we have progressed further than before. So from 1980-1991 the patterns took a specific shape and after that they went a little different from 1992-2003.

Now in 2004 we see nothing remarkable, which is expected. 2005 will be the start of the new patterns as it takes a full year for the energy to settle enough to be balanced and stable.

The solar cycle pattern previously discussed in plate 144a previously had a number of associations to research we were doing at the time and also showed us some interesting features which ended up correlating to many aspects of current research to do with Egypt and the pyramids at the time.

In this next pattern we see a solar flare depicted.

Crop Circles

Diagram 19.

This appeared on 14th July 2000 at West Stowell underneath Knapp Hill. This pattern represents a large solar flare!

July 14, 2000 -- This morning NOAA satellites and the orbiting Solar and Heliospheric Observatory (SOHO) recorded one of the most powerful solar flares of the current solar cycle. Space weather forecasters had been predicting for days that an intense flare might erupt from the large sunspot group 9077, and today one did. "Energetic protons from the flare arrived at Earth about 15 minutes after the eruption," says Gary Heckman, a space weather forecaster at the NOAA Space Environment Center. "This triggered a category S3 radiation storm."

Then there is this one!
Plate 11.

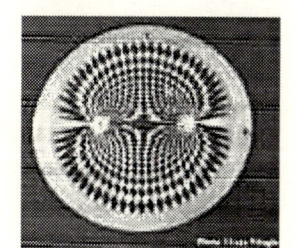

Appeared: 22nd July 2000. At Knoll Down nr Avebury Trusloe.

August 14, 2000 -- An interplanetary shock wave from the Sun struck Earth's magnetosphere just before the peak of the Perseid meteor shower on August 12, 2000, triggering a powerful geomagnetic storm. Stargazers across Canada and the United States were treated to the rare spectacle of a meteor shower seen against the backdrop of colorful Northern Lights.

Then there is this one from 2004!

Plate 12.

Some say it's a representation of a whole array of things from Mayan to Aztec. Many point to 2012. After spending a lot of time in this one it was man made and plenty of evidence to prove it. But as to whether its man made or not is not the issue here. It is simply why it is there and where did the so-called land artists get the detail from in the first place.

This scenario is much like trying to communicate to intelligent life out in space using radio signals. If they are

Crop Circles

more intelligent than us they would have figured out by now that there is a faster way to communicate over vast distances in space and radio waves are too slow.

So the chances of being heard whistling against the wind is negligible.

The same can be said for the man made or real argument. The issue is negligible. It simple comes down to what made them put it there and that particular design. If we are being communicated to by whomever then I am sure they would be able to make humans do things if certain factors were not right for the normal way to create the designs.

Humans have this attitude that they think they are smart and know about the universe etc. We are not the most intelligent life form in the universe and we are definitely not alone.

Evidence is all over the place you just have to stop and have a look around.

So! If we are being influenced to respond a specific way to the patterns then we need to find out what exactly is happening.

One instance was an experiment that we did back in 2001.

Taking line drawings of the designs we grouped them in sets of 8 and 16. Then when people bought them they reported that they were finding that headaches, backaches etc just disappeared after only having them in their pockets for 5 or so minutes. This was significant in that as they did not know what the experiment was about they could not have done it by their own thoughts. This led us to investigate further and found that the patterns were having a healing effect. Further investigations showed that a Japanese group had experimented with crystals and photographed them under an electron microscope before and after and after the quartz crystals had been placed on a line drawing on a piece of paper the crystalline structure had altered after being placed on the drawing. This meant that the geometric shape had an effect! So now the question is what creates the energy? Is it the geometric shape itself? Or is it a combination of inner geometric shapes that combine together to form the energy that is a crop circle.

The answer is a combination of 2 compatible sounds that when unified create a helix that forms from the intertwining of the two, thus the result is a visible helix type dna structure that has both a geometric shape at the base which will alter and be more complex the higher the compatible sounds are, plus within the loops of the helix is zero gravity.

This experiment was done at a university in USA in a sealed smoke filled chamber. The helix was plainly visible to the naked eye. They placed a small stone within one of the loops of the helix using a robot arm and it just stayed there within the loop. When the sounds were shut down the stone dropped to the table.

In this next crop diagram we see a depiction of the technique of 2 sounds combined to create a 3rd wave, which is used for communication.

Plate 13. It is the top end of this glyph that caught our attention!

Crop Circles

It clearly shows a device that uses harmonic convergence principles in a balanced form to emit a signal that could travel over a vast distance using what we call the "Unipulse theory!"

Crop circles have adapted over the years and now are far more complex than earlier designs. In the above design we see a number of elements that depict a Silica based lifeform as well as transmission techniques using harmonic pairing of sounds that give access to the unipulse system so you can transmit over vast distances without relying on radio waves!!

Early Egyptian mummies have revealed a deposit of silica in the sub cutaneous skin tissue. Plus experiments with harmonic compatible pairs of sound produce a helix energy that is the combination of the two which forms a helix which could carry a message over vast distances instantaneously.

Universities in USA have already run these experiments.

So the Chilbolton glyph is not as far fetched at it seems!

Negative Media

Well it certainly does not help, but it does not hurt either, as there are many ways of getting the message out there!

We have to remember that one important principle with crop circles is that they need to be seen. It does not

Jonathan Sherwood

really matter what label is on them as long as people sight the designs one way or another.

It is amazing what lengths some media and film groups will go to to try to get their way. In one instance they flew a group of hoaxers all the way to New Zealand to do a pattern in a farmers field there just so it would be away from the other researchers, and even then the hoaxers made a complete botch of the job.

Here is what happened as reported to us by contacts we have in New Zealand as well as newspaper reporters we contacted there.

March 1998 and 3 so-called circlemakers traveled to the southern end of the South Island of New Zealand near Winton. According to them they did it and simulated a night time pattern making session.. Oops! Sorry guys but I was raised down in those neck of the woods.. Dam! That means I have contacts down there!

The pattern was done under floodlights and the first pattern they had to abandon due to errors etc. After requesting another field from the farmer they then took around 8 hours to complete a pattern that was only 300ft across again under floods.

This is another example of cover up by media and folk like NBC etc.

You have to give em points for trying though...

This is an extract from the report:..

The assistance of other local people had also been much appreciated. Ascot Park Hotel manager Peter Ridesdale loaned a caravan, which was used as a control centre during

the all-night shoot involving crews from Queenstown and Wellington. Two 40-tonne cranes from Southland Crane Services were used to haul in and lift the powerful lights needed to film the all-night shoot. Helicopter Line

Crop Circles

pilot Dennis Edgerton provided the aerial filming platform. The original Friday night shoot had to be abandoned because of heavy rain, which forced the production to move to a second paddock for a second attempt on Saturday. The programme is scheduled for showing in the US in early May with release in New Zealand through TVNZ about six weeks later.

Note the comment they had to abandon the project. You do not have that luxury in UK the patterns appear rain hail or shine!!

What you do not see reported is 22,000 gallons of water disappearing from rice paddies in Japan and a crop pattern appears at the same time the water vanishes in the rice paddy field and 100 witnesses watch the event. Time involved around 30 seconds!

Nor do you see reports of tops of full-grown trees bent at right angles the top 30 feet bent to depict a crop pattern in Canada.

Nor do you see reports of crop patterns in deserts where the sand is fused into glass at the base of the trough that forms the ring.

Or maybe we should mention the errors that the so called hoaxers make and they leave it and go away for breakfast and then revisit the pattern only to find no sign of the error and a completed pattern.

Or how they lose 3 hours and have a completed pattern in front of them.

None of these stories are reported and yet it all happens!!

Jonathan Sherwood

Inside Crop Circles
The First Step.

Hidden dynamics within a crop pattern have had remarkable effects in a variety of ways over the years, from healings to improved memory to rejuvenation and reduction in aging. The list is endless. However what we have found over the last few years gives rise to speculation that there is more to these designs than first thought.

In 2001 we developed the analysis cards, sets of 8 or 16 line drawing copies as shown in the next diagram.
Diagram 20.

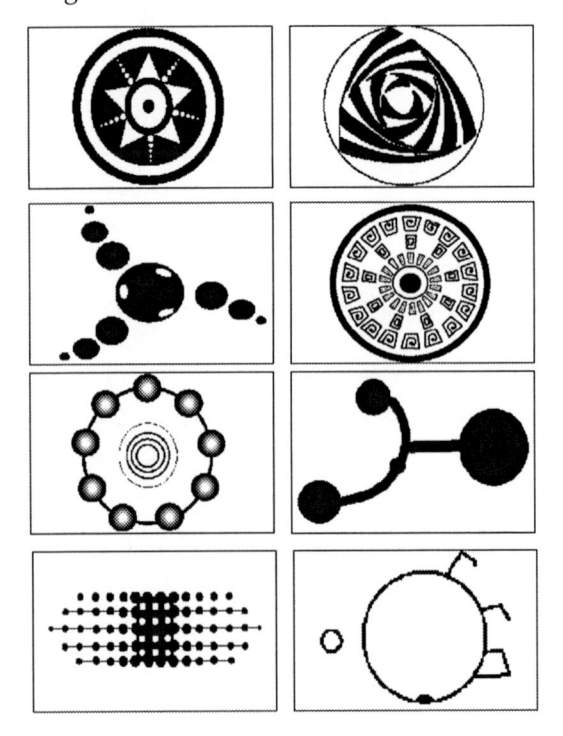

Crop Circles

These are nothing more than line drawn copies of original crop patterns and yet when they are grouped in sequences of 8 or 16 they have some amazing results. What is even more amazing is when done in trials people were not told what they were for. They just picked them up bought the set and them came back to report what was going on so no autosuggestion of any kind was involved.

It slowly became more obvious that the geometric shapes in certain types of harmonic groups had more profound effects than others. Work is still continuing in this area as of 2004/2005.

We know that geometric shape carries energy and can and does magnify the energy that moves across the surface of our planet. It is this force which gives rise to further speculation that if we begin to look at the complex geometric patterns now appearing in crop designs then we can surmise that as the designs become more complex then so too does the energy resulting from them.

In Japan for instance tests were done just on simple line drawing copies of original designs on flat pieces of paper. A quartz crystal was photographed under an electron microscope to gather an image of the crystals crystalline structure before placement on the line drawing. The same was also done to a second crystal, which was also placed on the same bench but not on a line drawing.

After 24 hours they were again photographed under the microscope and it was found that the crystalline structure on the one on the line drawing had altered whereas the one nearby on the bench had not changed!

After numerous tests over the next few days and weeks the same result always occurred. This showed that the line drawing itself was emitting an energy that could affect the crystalline structure of a known element.

If geometric shape can have these types of effects then we seriously need to better understand what geometric shape in other structures can have both on our own human health as well as other areas.

We also know from reports that people who suffer from Parkinson's and other debilitating illnesses stop shaking as in Parkinson's when inside certain crop patterns. All it would take is isolating the energy frequency that is within that particular design and use it to repair the damaged area of the brain as in all cases the Parkinson's sufferers did not have any attack for 24 hours after being in the pattern. Again it must come down to the energy within the design.

Plate 14.

Each design has its own unique signature and once this signature is understood then we can go further in our understanding of this simple principle that seems to be lost in modern day scientific study. And that is exactly what it needs, serious scientific study into the secrets of the geo energy principle behind geometric shape and how it affects us all.

So what exactly do we presently know about this first step in understand the inner mysteries of the Crop Circles.

Well we know that binary language is coded in groups of either 8 or 16 characters and that the ancients knew about this many thousands of years ago. There is even evidence to suggest that these same ancients knew more than we do today regarding the secrets of geometric shape and design as it can be found in many areas of ancient temples all around the globe.

So why do we have a hard time accepting that ancient tribes know more than we do and how can we learn from this?

The answer is simple! Look at it! See the crop patterns for what they really are, a learning tool to take us beyond our own limited methodologies and linear thinking processes, and try to understand that all things are created equal and no two aspects are better than the next! Crop patterns have a diversified range of knowledge that goes way beyond mere geometric language. As a philosophy they teach understanding of ourselves as the first thing you will do upon entering a design is become one with your own feelings in any number of ways. Now! When was the last time you did that?

And let's face it that is the first step to becoming self-aware!

Jonathan Sherwood

Hidden Design

Internal structures of crop patterns are both complex as well as dynamic. The energy that is formed inside a pattern builds over the first few hours after forming and only releases when it is at a certain level. This works much like a pressure cooker and energy is collected and magnified according to the internal geometric shapes within the design.
Diagram 21.

This design for instance will magnify and bounce the energy around inside itself until it reaches a release point then of it goes up as well as out laterally.

Whereas this one..Diagram 22.

has a totally different effect and magnifies in a totally different process. Firstly depending on how it is aligned will have great bearing on how well it works. If the design is in line with the earths energy field on the grid surface then it will enter the first part of the design bounce inside and magnify and then release down the pathway to the next section which adds to what has already happened, and so the process progresses until it reaches the end section and then the whole pattern is working. More complex segmented patterns like this

Crop Circles

one and those even more complex are called combination patterns or glyphs.

Plate 15..

Turned up in Avebury in 2004 and was aligned on the North/South axis. In line with the energy it started on the left of the picture and progressed through the design magnifying the energy as it went. The small stream of dot circles on the far right was where the most energy could be found. The largest circle 10th from the left had dual spin centers and the energy was doubled in this part of the design. Energy dynamics remember are not yet understood by many and you have to understand that energy when it interacts with geometric shape does have significant effects on a variety of areas from health to awareness and increase in mental function to environmental conditions. This design used a linear energy direction. In other words it kept the direction flowing North/South. Whereas in this next example we see a spin oscillation formed by the design.

Jonathan Sherwood

Plate 16.

In this design we see a number of variables. Firstly the outer area is made up of 16 surfaces, which would interact with the energy flow on the grid as it interacts with the shape. This means the directional energy once entered into the subsurface of the design will change direction and due to the amount of surfaces it will magnify faster plus it causes internal oscillation. The internal circular design is as you can see made up of dozens of curved and straight lines within another design and has 4 sections inside it. This magnifies the energy interaction 10 fold thus causing an emission of energy greater than most.

Crop Circles

Plate 17.

Even though we know that this one is man made the fact remains it is here and did have a variety of effects.

No matter how it got here the questions remain..
1. Why did the hoaxers choose to place the pattern right where they did?
2. Why that particular design?
3. Why that particular shape and size?
4. Why on that particular day?
5. Why at that particular time? Let's face it they would have had some form of communication and thoughts after all especially human ones are susceptible to telepathic impression. So it would not take much to make a hoaxer who is already geared to do something do what you wanted if you had the power.

So where does that leave us?

Jonathan Sherwood

Well humans are not the only intelligent life forms in the universe, and if we think we are then we have an ego problem!

Our ability to understand scientific values that are 500 years ahead of where we are at present is only limited to our understanding of those principles and our willingness to get to know more about it.

The crop circles have many inner messages if we are prepared to have a look. But remember that those messages will become more complex as time goes by. Simple circles like this one in the beginning can be accepted easily.
Diagram 23.

While one like this next one will take more time for us to accept that it could have happened for real!

We can only accept what we feel we can accept and to accept that many of the patterns are man made is easier to accept than the concept of alien contact!
Plate 18.

Crop Circles

This Mayan glyph type design as many have now called it appeared over 2 nights. Not completed in the first night, the design first looked like this!
Plate 19.

As you can see much of the detail is missing just the outline is there!

There were a number of patterns in 204 that took a few nights to appear.

This next one took 4 nights to get it all right!

Plate 20.

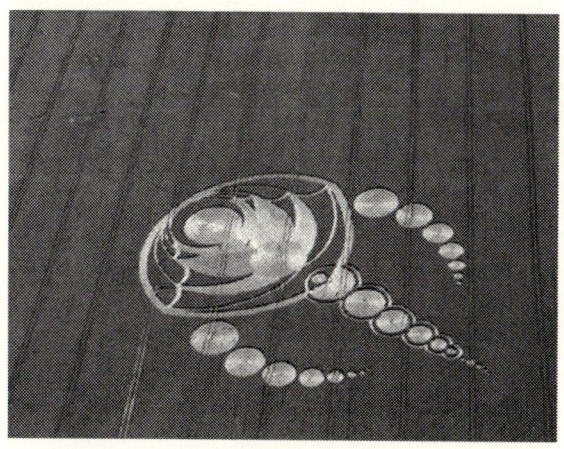

This is how it ended up after 4 nights.
It first looked like this!

Jonathan Sherwood

Plate 21.

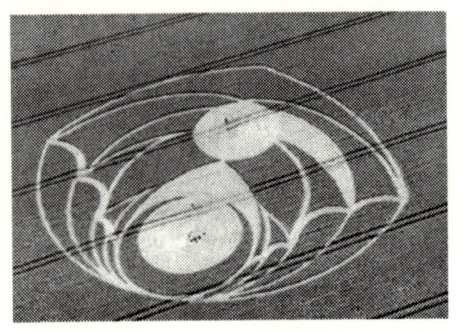

So we see that in the man made art arena they require at least 2 nights to get it right.

And yet this one arrived in just 15 minutes in 1996.

Plate 22.

The internal design of these amazing patterns will cause questions for years to come and we still have a long way to go to understand the inner workings of these geometric shapes.

Pattern connections to Ancient Sites.

There have been many comments regarding the purpose behind many of the ancient sites like Stonehenge, Avebury and others.

Over the years we have found that in ancient times unusual events were marked always by a ceremony or structure. Even religious mosques like the one at Luxor temple in Luxor Egypt was built on another older mosque type structure, which was also built on top of another.

Some areas in the world are classified as sacred and yet are not fully understood today as to there significance as to why that particular spot on the planet.

One example of early events of crop patterns arriving could have been the result of the eventual building of structures like Avebury and Stonehenge as the mere arrival of the pattern would have been interpreted as a sign from the gods so the area is blessed.

It would therefore be obvious for the ancient priests of the time whether they be pagan or otherwise to build a temple to mark the event. Or the gods had chosen the sight for the temple.

Either way the question remains as to why they were built on those particular points on the earth's surface.

Speculation abounds and yet, who is to say that crop patterns had been around thousands of years ago. There is plenty of evidence which points to the events taking place. We also have to remember that interpretation back then would have been totally different from what we know of today. I mean imagine them explaining the arrival of something like the Concorde back a few thousand years ago!

Jonathan Sherwood

We know from experience that crop patterns have appeared in the desert sands next to the pyramids at Giza in Egypt.
Plate 23.

They have also appeared by Stonehenge and Avebury as well as other sacred places all across the globe. Coincidence? I do not think so.

For instance if the Maoris of New Zealand can prove that they originated in Egypt and as they have not had any written language they used symbolic form to communicate.

Recently in 2000 the Maori elders released a number of ancient stories and information that had been kept secret for many hundreds of years, it confirmed that they could indeed prove where their origins began.

If our very ancient ancestors also had no written language but used geometric form as a way to communicate then the crop patterns suddenly have a new meaning that we need to interpret. Even the early hieroglyphic language is a pictographic geometric art form.

Language can take many forms and we need to explore the possibilities as to why these patterns are so mysterious and important.

Crop Circles

Regardless of who put them there or why we have to take into account the possibilities that telepathic communication has been a part of the equation for some years now.

Why?

Because if the energy that assists in creating these designs is somehow damaged in the past then another means of creating them would have to be applied.

We know from research that nuclear explosions do affect the energy field that is the grid around the planet. Blowing holes in it will only degrade the system further than it already is.

So it was good that all nuclear testing was stopped gives time for the grid to be repaired.

Many ancient sites like Stonehenge are located on this energy grid and most crop circles also appear at specific locations on the grid. This is more than coincidence and location of certain patterns appear to be in a circular zone that holds many interesting connections. The area for instance between Stonehenge and Avebury have had most of the largest patterns that have arrived in England. This points to an area that has some interesting features. The fact that there are many underground aquifers in the region is not the main issue. Geometric pattern in the landscape also plays an important part and is significant in that certain boundaries are at play. For instance Avebury is at the northern most boundary to a ring that has a southern boundary at Stonehenge.

Jonathan Sherwood

Plate 24.

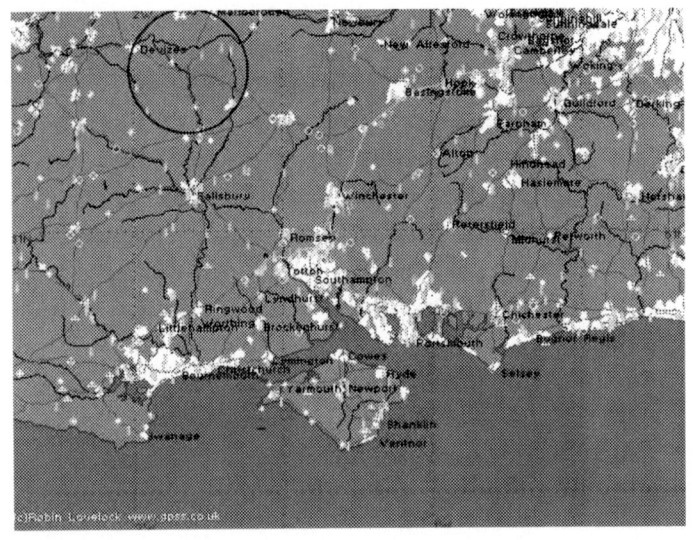

The circle on the map shows where the ring is and within that area most of the major crop pattern events have taken place.

Presently one can only speculate as to why they mainly occur in that region but it obviously has to do with grid energy and the fact that both Avebury and Stonehenge are on energy grid cross points.

Interestingly enough so too are all of the major ancient sites like Pyramids in Egypt, Pyramids in Mexico and also places like Machu Pichu in Peru. There are many more but these sites were strategically located there for a reason. And that is to tap into this ancient energy grid that powers these ancient sites through an advanced understanding of geomagnetic geometry.

Plate 25.

Effects

It is interesting that there have been many effects reported from people regarding their own personal experiences in a crop pattern. These effects vary from medical to physical phenomena.

Jonathan Sherwood

Plate 26.

This one made many people ill after being in the design.

While this next one even though the farmer destroyed a large position of it before many could enter it had the effect of disorientation.

Plate 27.

Like the temples in ancient Egypt, which incorporate a system of vertical columns of specific size, such as the Colonnade at Karnak in Egypt seen in the next image.

Plate 28.

Geometric stylized shape was important to the ancients and is just as important in crop circle design.

Influence is everything. The bigger the influence, the better the result.

Jonathan Sherwood

Diagram 24.

This one for instance was 1500ft across in undulating field. People entered and were affected in a variety of ways by this deign. Backaches disappeared to migraines and other conditions just seemed to clear up.

This next one appeared at Honey Street in 2000 and had the ability to create a silence while you were inside it, you could not hear any sound out and about. But when you stepped out of the pattern you could hear birds singing, crickets and helicopters flying about but inside there was no sound.

Diagram 25.

The ground anomalies with many of the designs take on new meaning when actual time is distorted as well and in many cases this has happened.

A variety of effects occur in any given geometric shape and that is caused by the energy ratio within that shape. Both angle, dimensions as well as position have a major bearing on what happens within any given architectural shape be it a skyscraper to a humble small shed.

Crop Circles

Just like when you walk into some buildings you feel uncomfortable or nauseous, so too do these effects occur in crop patterns. Many people feel sickly or nauseous when they enter certain patterns. Why? Because the energy that is present in there is higher than the individual in question. This means that your brain does not have the ability to analyze and cope with the higher frequency so you get a sickly or nauseous feeling. Bit like being on a merry go round. It disorientates thus causing a kind of vertigo in some cases. All the product of high frequency energy impacting on the brain, which cannot identify what, it is, as it does not have the ability to tune that high. This is similar to a radio trying to get a signal that is broadcasting at a range above what the radio tuner can reach. Interestingly enough research has shown that if you access a combination of patterns say 8 or 16 in any one season then you adapt and people seem to go through some sort of life changing experience shortly afterwards. This we think is due to the brain being reprogrammed to a higher level thus giving the individual a chance the make significant changes both outside themselves as well as inside. Health wise.

Jonathan Sherwood

Plate 29.

Our ability to understand higher brain function is brought about by experiences but what if those experiences were forced in a specific direction to stimulate growth.

Images like this one which appeared recently in 2004 of two dolphins orbiting a central design which symbolizes another design which affects time could be telling us we are running out of time. Again we have to remember that even though certain patterns were seen to be man made the design parameters could and probably were passed on by a higher force to the individuals to create the design due to bad energy in the area to a whole host of other problems that could have been present. We have to remember also we are messing up our own planet on a grand scale and have this crazy attitude that because it has always been there it always will be. Sorry but unfortunately it does not work that way. We are responsible for the planet and everything on it. Kill it off and we kill ourselves and where do you spend all the profit then eh!

Crop Circles

Diagram 26.

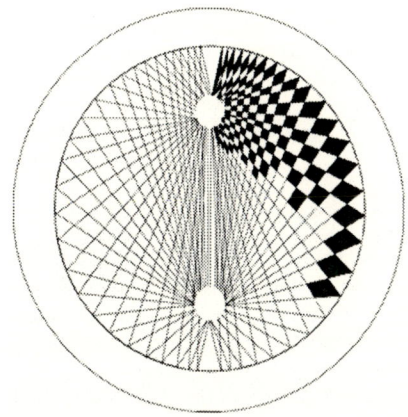

This is part of a scale drawing of the geo energy crop pattern that appeared in 2000. This particular design was interesting in that it had effects on weather and other elements.

Plate 30.

This is an aerial of the full design.

I think its time to have a deeper look at the geo energy system of the crop circles.

Jonathan Sherwood

Geometric Architectural energy principles

You could say that architectural style is also geometric shape. After all both are the same and use the same principles of size relative to dynamics. The problem is if you have not worked out the geo energy principle relative to architectural shape then you do not know or understand what you are creating energy wise within the shape or architectural design.

In example next we see a simple box shape. Measurements using the harmonic equation to convert mathematical shape into energy type show us that the energy type for this box shape is a high range harmonic that can assist to conclude events and also open new ones. This is important as it also shows that anything within the shape must be well controlled.

Diagram 27.

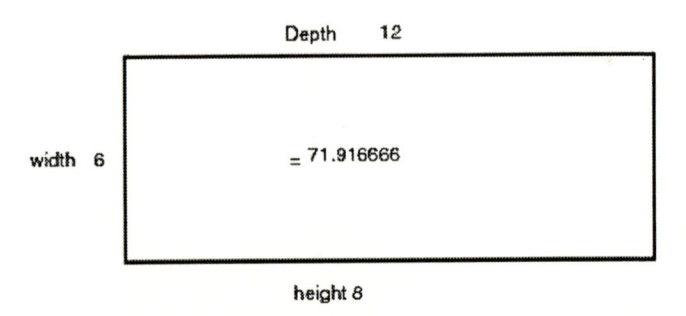

```
                    Depth    12
            ┌─────────────────────────────┐
            │                             │
 width  6   │         = 71.916666         │
            │                             │
            └─────────────────────────────┘
                    height 8
```

In this next geometric shape we find something else at work. This is a simple example, as we do not want to get too complex at this stage.

What we see is the addition of internal rooms.

Crop Circles

It's the dynamic shape and size of these rooms that changes everything within the main shape.

Diagram 28.

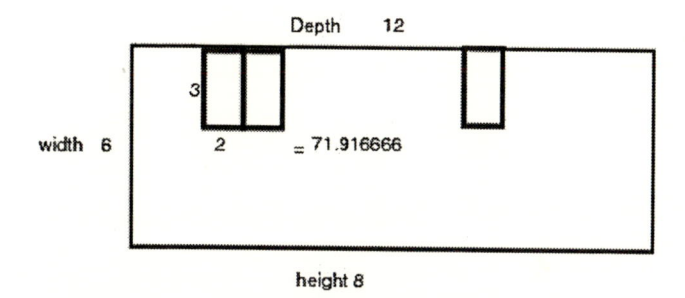

Depth   12

width   6   2   = 71.916666

height 8

So these same principles apply to crop circle patterns as well.

Plate 31.

This one has internal shapes that affect the initial energy of the main shape.

This means the energy dynamic has been added to thus giving the overall design a unique signature. The more complex the inner workings the more dynamic the energy will be.

We know that there are three energy types in a 3 dimensional space. So to make it simpler we devised a system

65

Jonathan Sherwood

that helps us to identify these three types in a mathematical formula.

A=.3333

B=.6666

C=.00 or integer series.

Now to work out this energy system in a mathematical way we also discovered a way to apply mathematics to work it all out.

First take the dimensions of the box earlier.

Height = 8

Width = 6

Depth = 12

Now any numbers more than a single digit reduce to a single digit by adding them together such as the 12, which means 1 + 2 = 3.

Now we have 863/12=71.916666

Now take that number and divide it by 12 which is the primary number that works with the equation due to its ability to reduce to 3 which is a primary number.

i.e.: 3,6,12,24,48.96.192 etc.

It also represents the universe in a mathematical formula of 3x4 = 12 dimensions making the combinations of 4 x 3 parts. This means we quarter the circle or bubble into 4 portions of 90 degrees each. This simple means 3 dimensions per part. So each part is 30 degrees. So 30 degrees by 12 equals 360 degrees.

Much like our own bodies are divided into 4 quadrants, front left, front right, back left and back right.

We measure distance relative to what we can see but not by what we feel.

Light travels at 186,000 miles per second and yet thought travels much faster but we have a hard time accepting that theory because we cannot see it!

Crop Circles

If the secret of three-dimensional energy is to incorporate 2 aspects of it to create the 3rd, which gives access to the other parts, then we can see where this could go!

Crop circles give us a sign that if we understand the physics of dimensional energy then we need to study the geometric energy influences further than we do.

The first basic step is this:
Diagram 29.

○

This is a single energy frequency (lets call it that for the time being)(It's actually a sound wave!) On it's own it is the first part of 3 dimensional space.

In order for the accessing of other dimensions you need to create a window to communicate.

This is done, by finding a compatible sound pair that can be identified. This must be done through a matrix, which we have the formula for.

Then we end up with two parts compatible.
Diagram 30.

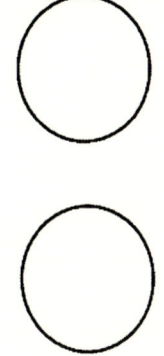

○

○

Jonathan Sherwood

Now we have two parts we need to bring them together so that they can create the third and most vital part.

Now in order to make this work an emission from both parts must take place at the same time. When this is accomplished you do not get a merging effect but rather a rapping one thus:
Diagram 31.

As you can see we now have a helix strand, which is the third and final link element. Two cells if you like that have been attracted by a common element.

We have used both geometric shape and mathematics to explain a very simple universal mechanism, so we see the importance of geometric shape in how we understand the universe in which we live.

It is obvious that the crop circles are here to guide us onwards to a higher understanding of what we already know but if we are afraid to look we will miss the message.

So architectural geometric design is far more serious than first thought as it can affect the way we are, the way we react, our health and much, much more.

We have learnt from investigating the crop circles that every shape no matter what it is has an influence one way or another.

Crop Circles

We collect things that we like the shape of or buy a house because of its shape or buy a car or boat because of the shape and yet we do not know what that shape can do to us.

Geometric Makeup

Here we will explore the geometry in principle and see where it leads.
Diagram 32.

This is one of the basic principles in archetypal geometry. We have not added the other rings so that it can be seen as clearly as possible otherwise it would be a maze of rings thus!

Jonathan Sherwood

Diagram 33.

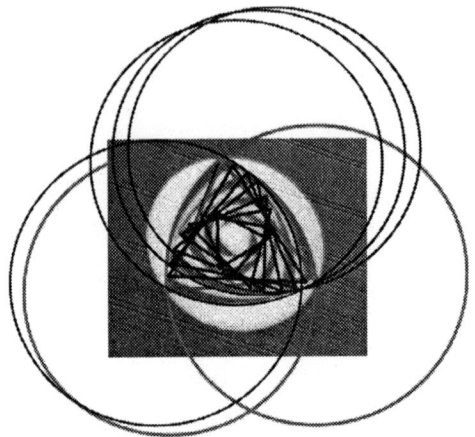

And even this is just a portion of the geometric makeup of this design.

Diagram 34.

This one gives us insight into a Spiro graphic type design with inlaid geometric portions.

Crop Circles

Diagram 35.

Diagram 36.

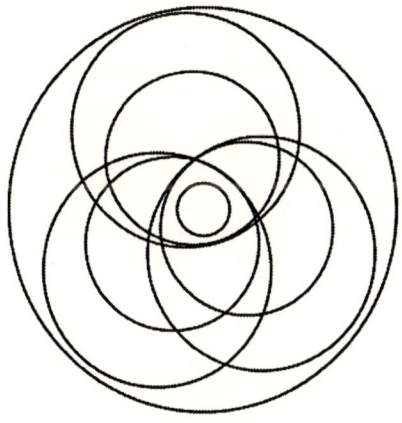

This design relies on circular center points to position the rings. If you look at the centers of each circle ring in the design you will see its center is positioned on a cross line from another for position.

Jonathan Sherwood

Diagram 37.

This is the result.

Here is another stage by stage.

Diagram 38.

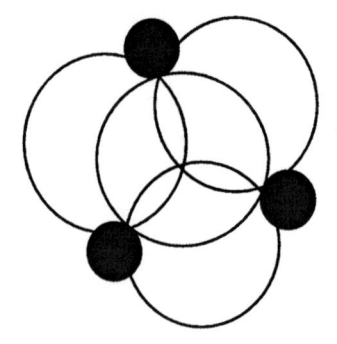

Crop Circles

Diagram 39.

Diagram 40

Each design is Geometry, which is done in a balanced way.
Diagram 41.

Jonathan Sherwood

Diagram 42.

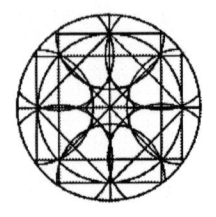

Diagram 43.

This is a good example of shape formed in patterning sections

Diagram 44.

Can you see the finished design that can be formed from this geometric compilation within the above pictograph?

Crop Circles

Diagram 45.

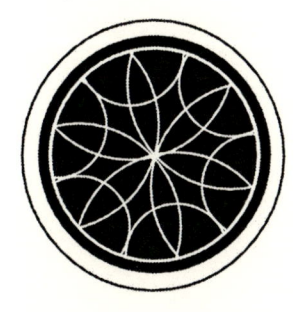

Diagram 46.

As you can see many of the designs are compilations of pictographic geometric states, which are then formed by filling in certain sections. An art form yes and complex to the point of having to think it out to create it and to get it on the ground in many undulating fields without distortions seen from the air would require adjustments on different scales relevant to the position of the design and lay of the land.

In the next drawing we see a more complex style, which requires a more precise alignment of the circles within it. This means that the centers of the circles had to be on a point whereby the space from one to the next could be measured.

Jonathan Sherwood

Diagram 47.

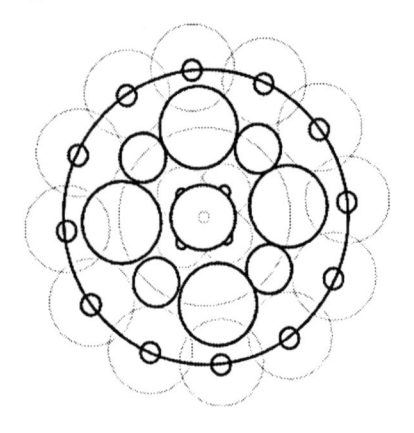

Diagram 48.

Plate 32.

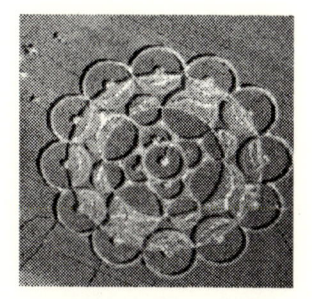

No matter how you look at he crop circles there is always an angle to consider or a geometric value to take into account.

Internal structures of the crop patterns are mostly simple geometry. In some cases they get technical, but still can be interpreted as fold type geometry.

In all crop circles can be easily identified as one of two things, man made or naturally formed. The man made events leave track lines in the pattern whereas naturally formed ones have no track lines. There are other areas that can be covered but one thing is for sure. More and more as the years go by we see more man made designs than naturally formed ones in UK.

This is all about to change from 2005 onwards as we enter into an energy cycle that is positive and will change the way we look at the world in which we live. Patterns will appear that are far more complex, but we have to open our minds to the immense possibilities of inner growth and a higher understanding of the influences around us from geometric shape and form, after all we live in a geometric world, we design geometric shapes that we both live in and use in a variety of ways and yet we are totally unaware of what sort of influences these shapes have upon our lives.

The time has come for humanity to see that science as we know it is only the smallest of drops in a very big ocean and we need to allow ourselves to see the entire ocean for what it is.

In crop circle geometric shapes it is not a case of how they got there in so much as to why they are there and what they say to us regarding hidden knowledge.

We all have to be prepared to look and allow ourselves to see that knowledge and not be blinded by what we think we already know!

Geometric shape holds the key to the energy of the future and the question is.

"Can we see it"?

The crop circles teach us a variety of things from geometric energy principles both in design parameters as well as shape and size dynamics. Then there are the healing properties of the shapes; this is of course relative to the design as to what each pattern does.

Then we have the inner effects on plants, soil samples, dna, human consciousness and the list goes on. So! Why do most people ridicule the designs? Because they are scary and unknown and yet these amazing patterns have the ability to help humanity to expand beyond where we are in such a way that our understanding of the universe in which we live would change forever if we understood just a small percentage of what these designs have to offer.

For instance how can 22,000 gallons of water disappear in a matter of a couple of minutes and a pattern appear in a rice paddy in Japan.

The ability to convert energy from water is presently not clear to humanity and yet here we see it actually in operation and it works. Imagine if we could do the same thing on such a scale.

Crop Circles

The concept of water conversion to energy is not that difficult. Conversion of the hydrogen content would leave just the oxygen so we would have hydrogen power. But this principle requires a modulated frequency that has the ability to separate the hydrogen from the water as was shown in an earlier chapter of this book.

The principle in the rice paddy goes way beyond this process as we see the entire water content disappear.

In every aspect the creation of an energy element requires the combination of two frequency elements that are compatible, once combined they intertwine thus creating a matrix which is the energy in a vortex form. This vortex form then consumes the elements in this case the water until it is completely consumed.

Once this has been completed we find a pattern in the field or paddy and that pattern is the geometric shape that has been created at the base of the matrix itself.

This shape is formed from the matrix or helix shape and with that shape are geometric dynamic forms all combining together. We see the helix form as we are looking from the outside on a lateral view. If you were to observe from above and also have the ability to see the geometric form at the base then the shape would also be seen. This would be possible by using sand particles at the base. This is also the reason why in many cases at the center of some patterns you find fused or molded glass from sand, as the energy would create the result as all the energy would be focused at the base at the last moment during the geometric shapes formation from the energies of the helix.

Now this might sound a little heavy going but the principles are not that difficult to understand once you get those basics we have just covered.

Jonathan Sherwood

The science of geo energy is not widely known but does exist in all things that have geometric shape.

About the Author

Dr. Jonathan Sherwood has researched crop circles in UK and elsewhere for over 10 years. Initially requested in 1994 to look at them. Dr. Sherwood has worked on developing ancient knowledge collected from all over the globe. He has appeared on TV and radio in USA, Australia, NZ, UK and also has been involved in Numerous documentaries on the subject.

In 1996 Dr. Sherwood discovered a harmonic energy formula that identifies energies within geometric from.

Working in UK he has researched over 300 patterns on the ground and has discovered some researchable information some of which is in this first book release on his work on crop circles.

Lightning Source UK Ltd.
Milton Keynes UK
174951UK00001B/20/A